The Act of
Consecration
of Man

More books by Tom Ravetz

Free from Dogma
*Theological Reflections in the
Christian Community*

The Incarnation
Finding Our True Self Through Christ

The Act of Consecration of Man

TOM RAVETZ

Floris Books

First published in English by
Floris Books in 2020

Unless otherwise indicated, Bible quotations
are from the New International Version.
Those indicated by A after the reference,
are the author's own translation

British Library CIP Data available
ISBN 978-178250-665-2
Printed in Great Britain by Bell & Bain, Ltd

Floris Books supports sustainable forest management by
printing this book on materials made from wood that
comes from responsible sources and reclaimed material

Contents

When the name of the communion service of The Christian Community was translated from the German *Menschenweihehandlung*, meaning Act of Consecration of the Human Being, in the 1920s, the word 'man' would be taken as 'human being'. In this book, I have tried to use gender-inclusive language. However, the title reflects the fact that our central service bears a name which some find outmoded. While liturgical language is not changed very often, we revisit questions of developments in the use of language at regular intervals.

Foreword

The celebration of the Act of Consecration of Man in community is the heart of The Christian Community. Its name enshrines its aim: the consecration of the human being. This connects to our experience that we are not yet everything that we could become. Created in God's image, our highest calling is to become 'friends', who will do greater things than Jesus himself (John 15:15). Along with the dignity of this calling, we experience the limitations that hinder us from answering it.

The opening words of the service are an invitation to everyone present to take part actively. This book is intended as a help in deepening that participation. If you are starting on your journey with the Act of Consecration of Man, you may find help on your path. If you have known the service for a long time, it may echo experiences and insights you have already gained and inspire further deepening.

Throughout the book, the following questions will be important:

* What experiences can we have in the Act of Consecration of Man?
* How can we deepen these experiences through preparation and reflection?
* How can participating in the service bring about changes in our lives?

Whilst *explanations* of the service tend to become dry and speculative, exploring *living concepts* that shed light on experiences can help us to deepen them further. The text is interspersed with *contemplations* that may help in individual inner work. They may help in preparing a space in the soul for more intense participation. They are inspired by Rudolf Steiner's remarks on spiritual training, above all in his *Esoteric Science*.

The book follows the structure of the Act of Consecration of Man with its four main parts:

* In the first part, the Gospel Reading, we hear the gospel of the week after prayers that prepare us for this. There may be a sermon. The Creed is spoken as a human response to the gospel.

* In the Offertory, we respond to the gift of creation by offering up the highest capacities of our soul to the divine world.
* In the Transubstantiation, we witness how Christ gives himself freely, imbuing bread and wine with his being.
* In the Communion we are nourished by the bread and wine which we receive as the body and blood of Christ.

At the beginning and end of the Act of Consecration of Man, special prayers ('epistles' or 'seasonal prayers') are spoken during each festival season. Between the festivals, a prayer to the Trinity is spoken (sometimes called the 'Trinity Epistle'). During the festival times further prayers are inserted between the main parts of Act of Consecration of Man.

The celebrant, an ordained priest of The Christian Community (man or woman), is supported by two lay people ('servers'), who represent the community.

Priests wear special robes when they celebrate. The black cassock is not visible during the service. Over this, they wear the white alb, a belt around their waist, a stole, which is crossed over the chest, and the chasuble, a robe with figures on the front and back. For the Gospel Reading, the chasuble is taken from the celebrant by one of the servers. For the Creed, the stole is taken off. The vestments and the antependium, the cloth that hangs in front of the altar, have colours that change with the festival season.

Seven times during the Act of Consecration, the celebrant makes the sign of the cross before their body, calling on the Father, the Son and the Holy Spirit. Anyone who wishes to give expression to their inner participation in the service is invited to make three small crosses in front of their forehead, chin and breastbone. These are the places where the consecrated substances are applied in the Sacrament of Baptism in The Christian Community. We can accompany this outer sign with the picture that as we make the three crosses, we are drawing the water of life that flows through the Act of Consecration of Man towards ourselves, entering the stream that flows over the child in Baptism (compare Rev 22:1).

Introduction

Opening

Let us worthily fulfil the Act of Consecration of Man.

One of the servers lights the candles and the priest and servers enter whilst a bell is rung three times to mark the beginning of the time that we will dedicate to the Act of Consecration of Man. The congregation looks towards the altar as the celebrant speaks the opening words of the service. At first it can feel off-putting that the celebrant stands with their back to us. With time, the experience may grow in us that we are all involved in the same activity, even though our roles are different. The congregation forms the back-space out of which the celebrant speaks. Members who have participated in the Act of Consecration of Man for many years describe how without conscious effort on their part, the words of the service take root in their souls and an inner speaking starts to complement their outer listening.

Sometimes words from the Act of Consecration of Man echo on in their soul in daily life, perhaps in a moment of need or as an inspiration when they speak with others. A reciprocal movement is at work: the celebrant speaks outwardly out of their deep listening; the outer listening of the congregation is complemented by their inner speaking.

In the course of the year, the Act of Consecration of Man describes how the divine word enters our soul. In the epistle spoken in the early morning on Christmas day, we hear how the word approaches human beings, touches our lips and enters our bloodstream. In the prayers that prepare the Gospel Reading, we pray that Christ's word may be in our hearts, from where it will issue forth in what is read. In the prayers at Eastertime, we are called to send the word out into the world, proclaiming Christ as the 'meaning of the earth' (see p. 53, in 'Words that make a difference'). Following this, at Ascension, we pray that we may be 'confessors unto' Christ. The word that we have heard and given space within us becomes our own word. Standing before the altar and speaking inwardly or outwardly to the divine world is an act of confession which makes the Ascension prayer real.

The question of who should be part of the church has occupied Christians for a long time. Often we categorise people into 'good' and 'bad' ones. What sort of people do we expect to find in the church? Should they all be 'good'? Then I might question whether I should be there. But are there truly 'bad' people there? Then I might find that I don't want to be part of it. I may be irritated or disappointed by someone who belongs to the congregation. Do I then have to leave this congregation and look for a new one, hoping that there will only be 'good' people there? It is even more complicated if I am out of sympathy with the priest, who has a leading role in the congregation. However, the great 'Let us!' includes all those present, without any conditions. With reflection, we may realise that our problems in community often have less to do with particular individuals than with the fundamental situation that we all have good and bad qualities, and that everything we do as a community is affected by this. My frustration with others is the mirror in which above all I can recognise myself. The image of a perfect community where I would not have to confront this uncomfortable fact is a fantasy, a refuge from reality.

Theologians have made the distinction between the visible and the invisible church. The visible church is the church that we know on earth, with its mixture of the best and the worst of humanity. The invisible church, on the other hand, is the ideal Church that will only be fully revealed at the end of time. In the Act of Consecration of

Man, we can experience that the invisible church is not far away in space or time, but that it becomes our present reality as the service goes on. This is echoed in the final words, which state with clear conviction that the service has been fulfilled. We have achieved something as a community that none of us could have done by ourselves. As celebrating congregation, we embody the reality of the Church in the here and now.

Every time we celebrate, the congregation is formed anew. After the Gospel Reading, the server, speaking for the congregation, refers to the one soul of the congregation which we lift up to Christ. Our souls have become one by being filled with the same gospel. At the beginning of the Offering, the radius of the circle of those taking part gradually expands beyond those who are physically present: it embraces 'all true Christians' and 'all those who have died'. At the beginning of the Transubstantiation, the celebrant speaks words that flow from the one heart of the congregation.

Words of prayer

Alongside their normal meaning, the opening words of the Act of Consecration of Man can be heard as a prayerful request: may it be granted to us to be worthy to perform the service. In the prayers spoken after the Offering at Christmastime, we join in the sacrificial hymn of the heavenly hierarchies, whose names are listed rank by rank. Some of these names are the ones we know from the New Testament and Christian theology. Some are given new names, which reveal more about their way of working. Every seasonal prayer gives a particular focus to something that is valid throughout the year. Every time we celebrate the Act of Consecration of Man, we stand before a world of spiritual beings and pray that we may join in their work. If we develop living pictures of these beings and their deeds, our experience in the Christmastime can grow all the more intense and our awareness of those who are joining us in the service can widen. This awareness can accompany us through the year.

First we can imagine the consciousness of those beings whose work is closely connected with the destinies of individuals and human communities. Many people live with the idea that they have a guardian angel who beholds the challenges and crises of their destiny, always sensing the opportunities offered by the challenges that they face.

When we widen our gaze to include the communities to which we belong, we can imagine the consciousness of the Archangels, which can encompass many individual destinies. The archangel sees in the challenges of our congregation, town or nation, opportunities for us to grow and develop in community. The Archai, or Time Spirits, are concerned with the destiny of the whole of humanity. Many of the things that disturb us when we read the news may represent opportunities for the spiritual growth of humanity in the eyes of the Time Spirit.

Each time we make the sign of the cross, we ask that the Holy Spirit might enlighten us: our limited consciousness is to become more and more one with his all-embracing consciousness. Angels, Archangels and Archai – summarised as the third hierarchy – work for this enlightenment in individual destinies, in the life of communities and in the history of the age.

When we turn to the beings of the second hierarchy, we encounter a consciousness that extends far beyond the destinies of human beings. These are the creator-spirits, whose work we see all around us. Rudolf Steiner, whose spiritual researches gave us an unprecedented level of detail about the working of the spiritual hierarchies, gave the beings of the second hierarchy new names, which allow us to see how they work in creation. Form, development and meaningful direction are the basic conditions for all development, and these are summarised in the names Spirits of Form, Spirits of Movement and Spirits of Wisdom. When we are creative, these beings are at work. We witness this in the Act of Consecration of Man: its clear forms serve its unfolding movement and life while everything that happens is irradiated by its clear purpose: the hallowing of the human, the consecration of man. When we call upon the Son-God to 'create in us', we can think of the beings of the second hierarchy through whom he works.

It is hard for us to imagine that aspect of reality that underlies all that comes into being and passes away. If in thought or meditation we can think away everything that changes and evolves, we will come in the end to Being itself. Everything that has come into being rests on the Ground of Being. When we live into images of the first hierarchy and their ways of working, we no longer have to accept the reality of existence itself as brute fact. Rather, we come to see it as the result of the sacrifices of the highest beings and their devotion to the intentions of the divine Father. Living with these thoughts can help us to hear the opening words of the Act of Consecration of Man all the more powerfully (see below: Looking with the eyes of hierarchies, p. 97).

Over time, we may come to feel that the two possible ways of hearing 'Let us!' merge into one. The great concern of the spiritual world is that the human be hallowed – they wish for nothing more than to see our progress to the next stage of our development. As a human community we join with spiritual beings who share our deepest purpose: the transformation of the world in and through the human being.

The contemplation opposite could be used as a preparation before attending the Act of Consecration of Man.

Contemplation: Two circles

I am sitting quietly before the service begins, surrounded by the congregation. I think of people who will probably not be present, but who know the 'healing power of the Christ'. This may include those who serve the goals of true humanity, even if they do not know the name of Christ.

I think of the community of those who have died who are known to me. I might think to begin with of those who took part in the Act of Consecration of Man during their lives. Then I extend the circle to include other souls beyond the threshold. I bring the question whether they are now looking for places of transformation in the life after death. I feel all these souls in a circle around me.

Now I look towards the altar, where Christ comes towards me. I imagine how the beings of the heavenly hierarchies surround him. Here the circles also grow in stages: from the Angels, who watch over individual human beings, to the Archangels, who take care of communities, small and large; from there, I imagine the spirit whose consciousness encompasses the whole of humanity living today. I imagine the work of the creator spirits, whose forces are at work in the Act of Consecration of Man with its clear forms, its movement and the clear purpose towards which it is directed. Then I try to imagine the beings whose sacrificial love is the expression of Being itself. These circles grow behind and above the altar, which marks the place where the circles of human and heavenly beings intersect.

I bring these images to life as vividly as possible in my soul. Then I let them fade away to nothing. In this nothingness I hear the words resounding:

Let us worthily fulfil the Act of Consecration of Man.

Act of Consecration

To consecrate means to make sacred or to dedicate to a higher purpose. In the ancient world, holy things had to be kept apart through a kind of ritual hygiene. Something of this lives on in us when we wait for a special occasion before we open a gift, or when we reserve the use of a certain room for special purposes. In the New Testament, however, a great change takes place: what is holy is now able to transform what is impure. Jesus embodied this new attitude towards holiness. He sought the society of ritually impure people, touched lepers and allowed himself to be touched by the sick. This went against the holiness laws of the Jewish religion. He explains this by saying:

> What goes into someone's mouth does not defile them, but what comes out of their mouth, that is what defiles them. (Matt. 15:11).

Although a kind of ritual hygiene is still necessary for certain purposes today, the tendency is clear: what has been made holy now has the power to transform the world.

Paul addresses the early Christians as the 'holy ones' or 'saints'. The first Christians experienced a consecration of their humanity through their encounter with Jesus Christ in their Baptism and in the Eucharist. When we celebrate the Act of Consecration of Man, we can have the same experience. This does not mean that we receive a status that separates us from the world. On the contrary, the Act of Consecration of Man connects us with the world in a deeper way, as it becomes apparent in the Communion (see Uniting with the world's evolving, p. 121). The holiness we receive in the Act of Consecration of Man becomes real when we dedicate ourselves to the purpose of consecrating the world.

The name of our service places it within the framework of the history of salvation. For the sake of their journey towards self-giving, creative love chosen in freedom, human beings had to be banished into a world of separation. They lost the holiness of their origin in this exile. Christ becomes human in order to consecrate the human being, to reconnect humanity to its divine purpose once again. In this sense, the incarnation of Christ itself was the original Act of Consecration of Man.

Christ in you!

Eight times during the Act of Consecration of Man, the celebrant turns around, makes a gesture of blessing and speaks to the congregation: 'Christ in you!' If we have started to experience that our inner word accompanies and echoes the words that we hear outwardly, these moments have a particular intensity. We echo inwardly the words that address us directly. The circle is completed when the congregation finds its outer voice after these words of blessing are spoken, and the server replies: 'And may he fill your spirit!'

At the basis of human community is our ability to share with each other what moves our souls. In modern times we have become accustomed to the definition of man as *homo sapiens*, the 'wise man'. Perhaps it is no surprise that this definition emerged in the time of the Enlightenment, when the lonely researcher in his study was regarded as the epitome of human progress. But knowledge without communication achieves nothing. It is our capacity to speak that makes community; this could be called *homo loquens*. This experience inspired the ancient mysteries of the word or logos, which later flowed into the logos-philosophy that grew up in the centuries before Christ.

Speaking gives our mobile thoughts form: a fleeting incarnation into a body of vibrating, moist air. Once someone has heard our thoughts, the thoughts exist independently of us. This everyday experience can serve to give us a picture of the divine logos, the primal principle of creation. Before the world was, the logos lived as thought in the mind of God. The whole of creation – the amazing variety of living beings, the unfathomable depths of the starry worlds, all the facets of human experience – existed as potential, as the unspoken word in the mind of God. Creation is the moment when thought becomes word: 'And God said, let there be light!' Everything that we see around us is a divine thought, which has taken on form in creation. In creating, the divine limits itself: only a part of the divine potential can be realised in the creation of the world.

The philosophers of antiquity regarded man as the third step of the logos into the world. Human beings bear the word as a seed within themselves. Our capacity for thought to understand the world comes from the same word-power.

We have already seen how the approach of the logos towards the earth is recapitulated every Christmas. The word is revealed as the light of grace in the midnight service; at dawn it touches us as the 'creator's healing word'. In the morning we hear the message that the logos has become man as Jesus Christ.

'Christ in you!' Is this sentence a statement or a wish? 'Christ *is* in you' or '*may* Christ be in you'? The fact that we can hear and understand these words rests on the power of the word within us. However, this word is not a voice that is constantly telling us what to do. Our lives would be quite different if we were always guided by the divine seed-word within us. To be human means to endure the tension between what we are and what we could be. The logos is waiting to be brought to life within us. In the Christ blessing, the word become man calls to the seed-word within us to new life. When the congregation finds its voice and replies through the server: 'And may he fill your spirit!' we witness the first fruits of this new life.

Contemplation: Trinity

The Father-God be in us;
the Son-God create in us;
the Spirit-God enlighten us.

In my imagination I peel away everything that covers over Being itself like the layers of an onion. Even the great mountain ranges, which can be seen as symbols of eternity, are in fact continually growing and passing away. What lies beneath all becoming, beneath all change and growth? The ultimate Ground of Being is the Father-God. I give thanks for this secure foundation, which gives me security in all the events of my life.

I direct my attention to the forces that keep me alive, far beneath my conscious control. I look back on my life. Everything that I am now is bound up with the mystery of my development, of my becoming. What kind of world would it be if there were no becoming? I thank the Son-God for this gift, which comes from his continuous, creative activity.

I become aware of the gift of my consciousness, without which this contemplation would be impossible. I notice how rich my experience is when I succeed in paying attention to the things that I see and the people I meet. I become aware that the connections that arise from this attention are the gift of the Holy Spirit and I pray that the Holy Spirit may continue to enlighten me.

Having pondered on these thoughts, which are themselves a starting point for many further ones, I may find that the mood of prayer stays with me. Finally, I let everything fade away. Into the silence I hear the words being spoken:

The Father-God be in us;
the Son-God create in us;
the Spirit-God enlighten us.

1

The Word of God:
the Gospel Reading

The Life of Christ

> But when he, the Spirit of truth, comes, he will
> guide you into all truth. He will not speak on his
> own; he will speak only what he hears, and he will
> tell you what is yet to come. (John 16:13).

The first main part of the Act of Consecration of Man, the
Gospel Reading, depends for its fulfilment on a counterpart,
a 'Gospel Hearing'. It is the work of the Holy Spirit that
connects listener and speaker. The angels are the servants
of the Holy Spirit – the Greek *angelos* means messenger.
The Gospel is called in Greek *euangélion* – the angelic
proclamation from the world of the spirit, the 'Good News'.

Long before we take in the details of any particular
reading, there is an underlying message in every gospel

reading: the divine world is communicating with us. The creation of the world is the first revelation of the divine, creative love, if we can read in the book of nature (compare Psalm 19). The incarnation of Christ, which lives on in the Gospel, is a continuation of this communication.

Everything that we experience leaves traces. Recent neurological research shows how every experience is inscribed in the brain. Connections are created between the synapses that are later available to our soul when we remember, in a way that has not yet been fully understood. Beyond this, what we speak and what we do is remembered by others. We carry within us the traces of what we have experienced, and we leave traces in our fellow human beings, if we have touched them in some way. These traces are real, even if we cannot touch them; we can imagine that they are the counterpart to a living world of experience, a sphere of memories that surrounds us, another layer around the earth, like another layer of its atmosphere.

When we remember someone who has died, we feel our way into this sphere. The counterpart of their earthly life remains in us as they find their way in the life after death. By living with our memories in an open way, holding our questions about the life that has come to an end on earth, we can deepen our relationship with those who have died. Our understanding of them starts to grow.

As this happens, we may find that we start to forget many details of our experiences together. Certain basic gestures of their life become all the more vivid when the firm outlines of the experiences gradually fade away. As time goes on, we may feel that we are getting to know new dimensions of our friend that go beyond what we knew during their lifetime.

Paul, who was a contemporary of Jesus, although he never met him, draws from two sources. On the one hand, there are memories of the life of Christ that were passed on to him by those who had witnessed them. Then there are teachings that he receives directly from the Risen One. Both sources are of equal importance to him: memory preserved by tradition and direct perception both feed into his main activity: *euangelisesthai*, preaching the gospel. The gospels had not yet been written down; Paul's preaching seeks to convey experiences to his listeners and readers, so that they can grow into the living sphere in which the deeds of Christ live on. John also refers to this sphere when he speaks of the impossibility of there being a book that could encompass all the deeds of Christ:

> Jesus did many other things as well. If every one of
> them were written down, I suppose that even the

whole world would not have room for the books
that would be written. (John 21:25).

The prayers that prepare the Gospel Reading lead us into
the sphere of Christ's life. When the gospel is proclaimed,
the life of Christ can come to life within in our heart.

The overflowing heart

My heart be filled with your pure life,
O Christ.

When we manage to listen to someone with deep attention, our soul grows still. We may receive insights as if in a dream, which we can then pass on to our conversation partner. Modern research has shown how such listening is connected to our heart. If we listen with our brains, seeking only to understand the thoughts of the other, the conversation remains superficial. If we wish to foster a culture of deep conversation, it works well if we encourage the conversation partners to attend to their pulse and to what they are feeling.*

The heart is an organ of perception for the other person. In the Old Testament the people of Israel are told ever and again that their heart has hardened. How can the heart become receptive again? In the Book of Deuteronomy (10:16), there is a powerful motif:

Circumcise your hearts, therefore, and do not be stiff-necked any longer.

---

* See for example this article from the Daily Telegraph: *www.telegraph. co.uk/science/2017/05/01/want-empathetic-listen-heart-beat-scientists-say/*

Circumcision is the ritual act through which a man becomes a member of the Jewish people. A wound has to be made in the body so that the bloodstream is opened for the spirit of the people to enter in. If we have an outer blockage in our heart, we have cause for concern. Nowadays there is a growing awareness of the inner blockages that can also afflict the heart. Marshall Rosenberg's method of nonviolent communication is one way of developing an awareness of this danger.* Ever and again we get into situations which overburden our feelings. We form a protective skin that shields us from what we have not been able to deal with. If we manage to pause for a moment and allow the dammed-up feelings to flow, something like the circumcision of the heart can happen. Doing this takes patience and courage. However, it is just through such openings that we become open for the other.

The Passiontide prayer speaks of the 'sting of evil' in our hearts. Might this sting, or 'prick', as it could also be translated, cause a wound to the inner heart? Then, this violent image would contain a promise of healing: after all, it is when we are vulnerable – when we can be wounded – that we are open to the world.

The seasonal prayers trace a journey of the heart through

* See Marshall B. Rosenberg, *Nonviolent Communication: A Language of Life*, USA 2015.

the whole year. The rhythm of opening and closing, receiving and giving, which is embodied in the beat of our heart, has its counterpart in the great rhythms of the year. At the beginning of the church year, we experience the receiving side of the heart, which feels the approach of salvation in Advent. It then feels the spiritual light in the prayerful mood of Christmas night. At Epiphany, the heart becomes active, radiating its warmth and love. The self-knowledge that we are called to develop in Passiontide tells us that our heart has grown empty. We have become 'heartless'. The shocking descriptions of the evil done in war and times of upheaval demonstrate what happens when human beings harden their hearts against the humanity of others. Populist politicians know that they will achieve their aims through what is called 'othering'. Only when we think that immigrants or the unemployed are other than really human can we accept the injustices inflicted on them. On a smaller scale, we may look back on times when we lost touch with our humanity. In the prayer which is read in Holy Week, the emptiness of the heart intensifies to an experience of burning, which we know as the fire of shame that arises when we allow ourselves to recognise how inhuman we have become by closing our hearts.

The Easter Epistle speaks of the empty tomb. Then, instead of directing our gaze to the garden as does the

Easter gospel, it points to the heart that is now filled with the life of the resurrected one. The heartbeat becomes a jubilant, healing power that praises the Spirit of God. In the further course of the year the heart develops a vision which sends out rays like those that stream out of the eyes of the angels in paintings by the old masters. At St John's Tide, the burning heart of the Passion transforms into the burning word of the Baptist in our hearts. The crowning of the year of the heart comes at Michaelmas. The source of the power that lives in the great 'Let us' at the beginning of the Act of Consecration of Man is revealed: Michael draws it from our heart. Now the heart may receive the Spirit into its glowing fire. All these images are in the background when we hear the prayers that prepare the Gospel Reading. Reflecting on our own heart-journey can help us to open our heart for the word.

Bringing the gospel to life within

We can deepen our experience of the Gospel Reading in the Act of Consecration of Man by living consciously with the gospels. There are many different ways of choosing what to read. We can start with the first chapter of the Gospel of Matthew and work our way through the gospels in the course of a few months. We can also take the weekly readings of the Act of Consecration of Man, either as preparation leading up to the next Sunday, or after hearing the reading for this week from the altar and perhaps having received some inspiration for working with the gospel reading through the sermon. Here I would like to highlight two ways of working with the gospels.

The *Lectio Divina* is an ancient method, which was developed into a system in the twelfth century. It has its roots in the theology of Origen (*ca.* 184 – *ca.* 253), who saw the gospels as a sacrament, an embodiment of the divine logos that we can perceive with our senses. According to Origen, meditation on the gospels can lead to an encounter with Christ.

for even in the scriptures the word became flesh that he might tabernacle among us. *(Philocalia* 15.19).

The *Lectio Divina* unfolds in four stages:

* *Lectio* (reading): we read the text out loud four times.
* In *Meditatio* (meditation or contemplation) we choose a verse or phrase that speaks to us. We try to understand it as deeply as possible. What is the meaning of the verse? What do the individual words and sentences mean? Are there echoes of other passages in the Gospel or in the whole Bible?
* If in the first two steps the word has spoken to us, the third step, *Oratio* (prayer) is about our answer. We experience the text in our soul and pay attention to what arises as a resonance in us. This can develop into a prayerful mood.
* In the *Contemplatio* (contemplation) we allow everything that we have built up in the first three steps to fade away, leaving only its after-echo, which gradually fades away as well. We dwell in this silence as long as we can.

The contemplation below uses the *Lectio Divina* to work with a famous passage from the Gospel of St John, which is sometimes called the gospel within the gospel.

Contemplation: God's love for the world

For God so loved the world that he gave his only begotten Son so that whoever opens their heart for his being might not be condemned to transitory existence but might have the life that endures into cycles of time (John 3:16 A).

After reading these words aloud four times, I ponder their meaning. I think of the divine love that is the foundation of all being. I think of the faithfulness of the divine world to a humanity that does not remember its origins in this love. I contemplate all the forces of evil and resistance in the world. What does the divine world have to suffer and endure in order to affirm the world in love? I feel how the incarnation of Christ is a further affirmation of this love: God does not behold the world from outside, but joins us in the midst of evil and suffering.

I contemplate the unusual translation, 'whoever opens their heart for his being'. What does it mean to open my heart to someone? I remember conversations in which I experienced this. I realise that the quality of belief that is conveyed by these words is far deeper than the weaker kind of knowing, which is often what we mean by belief. I try to understand what could be meant by 'the life that endures into cycles of time'. When do I lift my inner gaze above the narrow horizon of my present life? What fruits might our culture bear, which will last beyond the end of the current cycle of time?

Next, I feel my soul's response. Perhaps I have noticed how many of the problems we encounter in living and working together have their ultimate cause in the fact that so many people doubt whether they are worth something, especially if they have made mistakes about which they feel ashamed. How much pain might we avoid if we only realised that the question of whether we are lovable can only be decided between us and the divine world and that we don't have to burden anyone else with it!

I might try to feel the magnitude of the sacrifice of the divine world which gave us Christ; I might allow the reality of his suffering and death to fill my soul, even drawing on experiences with the gospel readings of Holy Week. I feel this sacrifice as a proof of God's love that truly embraces all people and all beings. Can I feel the depth of a love that even includes dictators and tyrants, paedophiles and terrorists? And last but not least: a love which includes myself?

All of these feelings might then turn into a prayerful mood: I pray that people will experience more and more that they are loved. I might apply this to myself or to people I know. Beyond that, I might think of those in positions of power whom I might easily dismiss as ambitious or driven by fear and imagine the love of God enfolding them as well.

Finally, I recall the verse once more. I allow the words to echo on in my soul. All thoughts, all feelings disappear again. I pay attention to the silence that develops in the centre of my soul.

Bringing the word to life

The following approach, which is often used in Gospel study sessions in congregations of The Christian Community, works well when we want to work with the weekly readings or pericopes (excerpts). These are the passages that are read during the Act of Consecration of Man, according to an order based on the festival seasons.*

* First, we familiarise ourselves with the passage by reading it a few times. It can be helpful to put the Bible down after each reading and then to reconstruct the steps of the story, perhaps with the question, 'What happened next?' Only when the order of the events or thoughts is clear in our mind's eye and we can recount it to ourselves like a storyteller do we move on to the next step.

* We then try to imagine the story, perhaps by visualising it being performed on a stage before us. This often leads to a multitude of questions that we can't necessarily answer. What sort of clothes did people wear in those days? Did they sit in chairs or recline on couches when they ate, as the archeologists tell us? What did a loaf of bread look like? We are not

---

* See Hans-Werner Schroeder, The *Gospel Readings in the Cycle of the Year*, available as a download *www.florisbooks.co.uk/freepdfs/*

aiming for historical exactitude. What is important here is to decide on an image, knowing that it can be corrected over time. Often we may notice that, previously, we were not really imagining anything, but shifting shadowy place-holders back and forth in our minds.

✳ In the third step, we imagine ourselves as one of the characters in the story and try to experience it from their point of view. At first we can imagine ourselves as a bystander – one of the crowd, perhaps, or a disciple who does not speak. It can be useful to imagine ourselves meeting a friend and saying, 'Guess what I saw today!' After this, we imagine ourselves as one of the main characters in the story, for example as the person seeking a healing. Finally, we can attempt in all humility to imagine the experiences of Jesus.

It works best if we bring each step to a conclusion well before starting on the next.

Contemplation: The blind man

As Jesus approached Jericho, a blind man was sitting by the roadside begging. When he heard the crowd going by, he asked what was happening. They told him, 'Jesus of Nazareth is passing by.'

He called out, 'Jesus, Son of David, have mercy on me!'

Those who led the way rebuked him and told him to be quiet, but he shouted all the more, 'Son of David, have mercy on me!'

Jesus stopped and ordered the man to be brought to him. When he came near, Jesus asked him, 'What do you want me to do for you?'

'Lord, I want to see,' he replied.

Jesus said to him, 'Receive your sight; your faith has healed you.'

Immediately he received his sight and followed Jesus, praising God. When the community saw it, they also praised God. (Luke 18:35–43).

Here are some questions that could be helpful in the second step:

* How was the blind man sitting? Was he holding a begging bowl in his hands?
* How can we imagine the group following Jesus? At the beginning of the story, the evangelist calls them a crowd. What kind of emotions are going on in the people who so confidently want to silence the blind man? What happens in them when he asserts himself again? What has happened that means that after the healing, the evangelist calls them a community? (Greek *laos*, temple community, where our word layman comes from)
* How did they bring him to Jesus? Roughly, or kindly?

For the third step, imagining the experiences of the blind man can make the passage come alive.

* What is it like to sit begging at the side of the road without being able to see?
* What is it like calling out loud enough to bring a crowd to a standstill with my question?
* What did the blind man feel when silence descended and Jesus called him to him?

* What was it like to walk to the front? Did the people he passed by speak? Did he feel their impatience?
* What does it feel like to hear Jesus' question? Does the blind man experience it as a further test of his resolve? How strong is his will to see again?
* What is it like suddenly to receive one's sight?
* What is it like to experience my healer as the very first thing that I see when my sight is restored?

Words that make a difference

Immediately after hearing the preaching of John the Baptist, his listeners asked him: 'What then shall we do?' (Luke 3:10). The first Christians felt the same. Bearing witness to the truth of the gospel meant embracing a radical change in their way of living and worshipping. This decision could have deadly consequences. Even in peaceful times, joining the church resembled an initiation with a long preparation, which reached its climax in the night of Holy Saturday. After confessing their sins and receiving an exorcism, the candidates undressed. They were immersed in the baptismal water three times. Each time they were raised out of the water, they were asked: 'Do you believe in the Father – in the Son – in the Holy Spirit?' Three times they answered, 'I believe!' in Latin: *credo*. That was the origin of the creeds as they are still recited in the churches today.

Following the Gospel Reading in the Act of Consecration of Man, the stole is removed and the celebrant appears just as they were when they entered the church for their own Ordination, which demonstrated their commitment to make their life into an act of confession to Christ. The Creed which the celebrant speaks after the Gospel Reading has a different character to most of the rest of the service. It is not a prayer but a kind of statement.

We do not ask that the Father *may* be the ground of being, or that the Christ *may* be his Son. Nor do we pray that the Holy Spirit *may* enlighten us. The affirmation, 'Yes, so it is!', is an affirmation of the celebrant's conviction, not a prayer. Reciting the Creed is more than an assent to particular facts: it is an act of faith, as this was understood in the time of Jesus. In the ancient world, faith was seen as a statement of loyalty and commitment to the spiritual world rather than an assent to facts that could not be grasped by the intellect alone, as it tends to be seen today. Such an attitude still lives on in terms such as 'faithful'.

If we live intensely with the gospel, we might find that the question: 'What can we do?' rises up in us. The Creed provides one possible answer: 'Bring the fundamental truths of Christianity to life in your soul so that you can bear witness to them in thought, word and deed.'

The Creed gives an outline of the history of the world as the story of creation, redemption and sanctification or consecration. A single, unitary divine being is both the origin and the destination of the world – the Ground of Being. If we explore the image of 'ground', we find that it is the foundation on which everything else rests. It can also mean the 'grounds', the reason for something. God, as the Ground of Being, spans world origin and world purpose. Affirming that this ground is 'spiritual-physical' challenges us to seek the archetypes and formative forces of what we perceive with our senses within it.

Developing our thinking to make this real for ourselves is a historic challenge. For centuries, human beings have divided the world in two in their thinking. This division first became apparent in decisions about the nature of God and the world that were taken by the Church in the fourth century. The world that we can perceive with our senses was declared to be outside the realm of divine creativity.* In the space that this created, the materialistic worldview took hold ever more strongly. The logic of materialism denies not only the idea of a creator-god but also the idea of their being any purpose or overriding direction in the process of creation and development. To recognise the Ground of Being at work in everything, to overcome every division in our thinking – that is the challenge of the first sentence of the Creed.

This has practical consequences. If we regard our practical duties as necessary evils, instead of carrying them out with attention and love, we are perpetuating the division. Living in alignment with the Ground of Being, or the Ground of the World as it is known in the Creed of the Christian Community, also means finding harmony with all aspects of our own being. If we accept this challenge, our prayers to the Ground of the World will become ever more substantial.

* See Ravetz, *Free from Dogma*, Floris Books 2009, p. 43.

When we try to imagine the eternal birth of the Son from the womb of the Ground of the World, our inner gaze turns from the world of Being to that of becoming. Birth is something that happens at a point in time: there is a before, when it has not yet happened, and an afterward, when it is over. The image of the eternal birth challenges us to embrace the reality of the Son of God, whose very being is becoming. The fate of the principle of becoming itself, when as Jesus Christ he encounters a world whose ideas and forms have become rigid, is summarised in the sentences about Jesus' birth, death and resurrection. Living with the gospels can help us to bring the short sentences of the Creed alive.

The final sentences summarise the working of the Holy Spirit. Many Christians who live with the image of the Trinity find it hard to describe the third person of the Trinity. Father and Son – these are images drawn from our experience of childhood. Spirit is more elusive. This very experience reveals something of his nature to us. He is the great connector, the medium that joins Father and Son in their eternal communion. When we contemplate the reality of the spiritual world; when we pray; when we turn our attention to the things of the created world, the great connector is at work in us. To acknowledge the reality of the divine world not only in thought but also in deed means that we willingly join in the great current of communication.

Participating in the Act of Consecration of Man is an act of confession. The more we inwardly accompany the words and actions of the service, the more this becomes so. In the Transubstantiation we ask Christ to bless this confession of the will. As we approach Communion, we make a twofold confession to the divine world. Before receiving the bread, we confess our situation as those suffering from the sickness of sin. Before receiving the wine we make a positive confession to Christ and to the Ground of the World that is revealed through him. Our work with the Creed can fill these moments with ever deeper meaning.

In the Easter prayers we hear a clear call to confess Christ's death and resurrection as the 'meaning of the earth'. Many people feel a certain shyness about telling other people about their spiritual experiences. We may have noticed how easily precious words such as God, Christ, or salvation can become mere phrases. However, we also encounter many situations in which the right word can be a comfort for people who feel overwhelmed by the apparent meaninglessness of their suffering or of world events. A gentle tact is needed here and we may wait a long time before naming Christ. But if we are attuned to others' needs and try with halting words to convey our conviction that meaning is inscribed deep into the fabric of all being, that failure and death can be the place of new life – then we fulfil our task of proclaiming the meaning of the earth. And even if we feel inadequate or have to experience rejection: is it not worthwhile to endure such petty troubles when we try to confess Jesus Christ, who died bearing witness to the meaning of the earth?

The Creed is spoken before a threshold that divides the Act of Consecration of Man into two parts. We could sum up everything that we have experienced so far as the service of the word. The seasonal prayer, Gospel Reading, sermon and Creed have revealed the reality of the divine world to us and called forth our response. With the beginning of the Offering, the Act of Consecration of Man passes over into deeds. After the Creed has been spoken, the chalice, which until then has been standing on the altar, shrouded with a cover, is unveiled for the first time. In the early centuries of the church, it was the custom in some congregations that those who had not yet been baptised and who had not yet made their confession were only invited to attend the Mass until the Gospel Reading. As they had not yet been initiated into the mystery, they could not take part in what happened after this. Today, the whole Act of Consecration of Man is open to everyone. There is however a further step for anyone who wants to connect more deeply with it and with The Christian Community: this is the step of becoming a member.

Membership

Making a public confession of faith was a powerful way for the earliest Christians to demonstrate that they belonged in the church. The link between the Creed and membership continues in a more inward way in The Christian Community. Everyone is free to attend the Act of Consecration of Man. If someone wishes to become a member, they are given the Creed to work with. In a church that makes no distinction between members and non-members in its worship, membership may seem superfluous. Perhaps the very fact that the offer is completely free gives it a deeper significance. New members often describe how their experience of communion deepens after they have made the step to membership. Their decision has given a form to their participation.

This comes to expression in the realm of rights and responsibilities: members are involved in decisions affecting the congregation in a more formal way than those whose relationship to The Christian Community may be deeply felt, but has not found a binding expression. Members may be asked to join a finance committee or congregational council. They have given a clear signal that they bear a concern and responsibility for the life of the congregation.

2

The Free Deed: the Offering

Near and far

Once the chalice has been uncovered, we turn to the Ground of the World, asking that our offering be received. We could only speak these words out of a trust that we are connected to the ultimate Ground of Being, who will hear our prayer.

In the next moment, we hear that the offering is brought by an 'unworthy creature', separated from the Ground of the World by an abyss. Some people struggle with this description of themselves as part of the co-celebrating congregation as 'unworthy'. For many centuries, the churches told people that they were sinful and guilty. The healthy, free human spirit rebels against such a picture. The struggle to gain a positive image of the human being, against the resistance of the churches, went on for centuries. Surely a modern church service shouldn't return to such old pictures?

If we look into our souls, we may find much that is worthy along with much that is not. As much as we can experience ourselves as creative, free and loving, we also experience fundamental limitations that stand in the way of this love, freedom and creativity. A picture of ourselves that embraced only one side of this tension would not do justice to our experience.

Owning our limitations can motivate us to live with them creatively and move beyond them. When we move out of alignment with ultimate reality, when we deny the reality of the spirit and when we allow our weaknesses to govern us, blockages form in our soul. As the first prayer of the Offering continues, we acknowledge that these blockages have already detached themselves from us and have flowed towards ultimate reality. We can experience this release as grace. When John the Baptist says of Jesus, 'Behold, the Lamb of God, who takes upon himself the sin of the world' (John 1:29 A), we can feel the threat posed by the consequences of sin to human beings and through them, the world. The word 'redemption' is drawn from the world of kidnapping and ransom. This image tells us that there were consequences arising from humanity's journey into separation for which we could not compensate through our own efforts.

Preparing for the first part of the Offering can help us

to experience it more deeply when we are in the service. The old theological concepts can be a help here, if we can free ourselves from their moralising overtones. Paul's letters contain 'catalogues' of sins that were summarised in the Middle Ages as the seven deadly sins, or perhaps more accurately, the capital vices.* Vices are deep predispositions which are beyond our conscious control. They make us susceptible to temptations that in turn lead to sin, which means that we incur guilt. Faced with the reality of our guilt, we may feel so crushed that we freeze up inwardly. Perhaps we cannot see any prospect of ever being able to put things right. Over time, however, we may realise that surrendering to despair is of as little use to the world as frivolously ignoring our strayings into sin and refusing to learn from them. In the moral theology of the Middle Ages, such despair is called *acedia,* which can be described as a spiritual laziness. However, the feeling of guilt can become the driving force of a renewed will to learn from life, as we have already seen in connection with the Passiontide prayers. Our responsibility is to review our mistakes so honestly that we can wrest from them every possible insight, in order that we can go back into life wiser and more compassionate.

* These are pride (Latin *superbia*), envy *(invidia)*, gluttony *(gula)*, greed *(avaritia)*, sloth *(acedia)*, wrath *(ira)* and lust *(luxuria)*.

The Sacramental Consultation gives us the opportunity actively to allow the blockages that have formed in us to flow to the divine world, so that we become receptive to the blessing that streams towards us during the service.* We may be aware of things we have said or done because of our limitations, or old ideas that we have developed in order to shield ourselves from aspects of reality that we do not wish to confront. When we prepare ourselves for the Act of Consecration of Man, we can ask ourselves what still burdens us, what has not yet flowed away from us to the Ground of the World. From such self-reflection we can also judge whether a Sacramental Consultation could be helpful.

Acedia, spiritual laziness or sloth, is a besetting challenge in our time, as we have seen above. It refers not only to our external duties, but also to the effort to recognise the reality of the spirit in every moment. Our culture's prevailing way of thinking still denies the reality of a spiritual world and limits itself to what the senses can perceive. Working with the first sentence of the Creed offers the possibility of consciously confronting this problem, as we saw above.

* For more information on the Consultation, see Ravetz, *The Sacramental Consultation,* Floris Books 2009, available as a download *www.florisbooks.co.uk/freepdfs/*

In our personal religious life this inner work on the consequences of sin can be helped by praying the Lord's Prayer, particularly the sentence about trespass or debt. The Greek word *aphes,* which is translated as 'forgive', originally meant 'to send away' or 'to let go'. When we prepare for the Act of Consecration of Man, it can be a help to reflect on the debts that we have incurred. These include the results of our mistakes, which come to expression in the word 'trespass'. We are also indebted simply by living in an interconnected world. What is it that needs to happen so that when I get up in the morning I can find electricity when I switch on the light, clean streets, people who will look after me if I get ill, and the infrastructure that delivers my food and water? These are debts that are incurred without my personal guilt. Awareness of this web of debt can help us if we become too preoccupied with the areas where we feel that others owe us something and with the wrongs that we feel that we have suffered. All this serves to deepen our participation in the Offering. In the chapter on Communion we will discuss the consequences of the sickness of sin in more detail.

Human work

Awareness of the gulf that separates us from the divine world can inspire us to offer up the positive forces of our soul. In the service for children in The Christian Community, the children hear that human beings are called to 'work in the world'. We have already looked at the alternative designation of man as *homo loquens,* the speaker. Philosophers have also used the designation *homo faber:* man the maker, the creator.

In the age of robots and artificial intelligence, the question of what the indispensable human contribution to the world might be is becoming increasingly important. If so much human work can be done just as well, or better, by machines, what remains that can only be done by human hands if it is to have its full value?* In the debates between theologians and scientists in the nineteenth century, some theologians sought to prove the reality of God as the necessary explanation for what the scientific view of the world could not explain. This argument was mockingly referred to as the 'God of the gaps'. If the theory of evolution by natural selection explains the development within the species but not the origin of the different species themselves, then this must the work of the Creator-God. There is a danger in putting our faith in such 'proofs': when

* See Yuval Noah Harari, The meaning of life in a world without work, *theguardian.com/technology/2017/may/08/virtual-reality- religion-robots-sapiens-book* (viewed 2/12/2019)

new research fills the gaps with more convincing theories, the space left for God shrinks ever more.

In the twenty-first century, we might ask whether we have arrived at 'the human being of the gaps'. The machines of the first industrial revolution replaced a lot of manual labour. Now the fourth industrial revolution, following on from the electrification of mass production and building on the digital revolution, is replacing human beings in areas of work in which their contribution used to be seen as indispensable. Much of what a solicitor does can be done better by artificial intelligence. Care services are increasingly performed by robots. If computers can compose works of art, pieces of music or poems that fool even the most experienced critics, what gaps will be left for the irreducibly human?

The words of a church service could be played back from a recording or recited by a speech synthesiser; the external actions could be performed by robots. Such a shocking idea makes it clear that the external movements of the vessels and the sounds of the words of the service would be meaningless on their own. It would be a grave error if we understood the strong ritual forms of the sacraments of The Christian Community in a purely mechanistic way. Without the contribution of human beings, the service would be nothing. This contribution is their inner participation. This can only arise in the human soul.

The gift

The whole of life unfolds in rhythms of giving and receiving. The simplest living beings take nourishment from their environment and release substances again after they have transformed them. Animals bestow life on their young through gestation and birth, giving of their own substance. They bring them food, even if this means that they themselves might starve to death as a result. Beyond what they share with plants and animals, human beings may freely decide to make a gift, even when there is no biological reason to do so. Even the earliest cultures cultivated elaborate rituals around gift-giving. One of the deficiencies of modern life is that many people are so isolated that they have no-one to whom they can give something. Fairy tales tell of the miser who, wishing to make himself secure, grasps at wealth for himself, only to find that he has nothing of value because there is no-one in his life to whom he can give.

From time immemorial, human beings felt compelled to give something that was precious to them to the divine world. When we read about the sacrifices in the Old Testament, we can sense the underlying conviction that the divine world will be enriched by the offering.

and you offer to the Lord from the herd or from
the flock a food offering or a burnt offering or a
sacrifice, to fulfil a vow or as a freewill offering
or at your appointed feasts, to make a pleasing
fragrance to the Lord (Num 15:3 A).

The Old Testament describes a path of development
that leads from outer sacrifice performed in the temple in
Jerusalem, to a sacrifice of qualities of the soul and spirit.
This is expressed very strongly in Psalm 51:16f:

For you have no pleasure in sacrifices, otherwise
I would give them to you; you have no pleasure
in burnt offerings. The sacrifices that please God
are a broken spirit; you, O God, will not despise a
broken and contrite heart.

In the second part of the Offering, we can feel ourselves
part of a sacrificial community that has existed since the
most ancient times. The sacrifice that is needed is now
entirely inward. Instead of a bull we offer up grape juice as
the bearer of our will; instead of a lamb we sacrifice water
as the bearer of our feelings. With the mixture of water and
wine, we offer up our thinking rather than a dove. These
capacities of our souls are our treasures. Even our outer

possessions receive their value through inner processes. Gold has no intrinsic value: only the will that it symbolises makes it precious. When the 'draught of health' in the chalice is offered up to the Ground of the World, we can feel that we are offering up everything most precious to us.

How can we make this offering real for ourselves? Reflection and preparation before the service can be a help in this.

To you be turned my willing.

We have taken time out of our everyday life in order to attend the Act of Consecration of Man. Our active participation is an act of will, all the more because we are not required to do very much outwardly. Through this act of will, we can offer up our feeling and thinking.

... feeling that unites with Christ.

Feelings can be like the weather of the soul: they rise up and disappear, and in normal life we exercise little control over them. If our feelings are to unite with Christ, we need to bring them under our conscious control. Living with the gospels in the way we have looked at above, is one way of schooling our feelings, and the contemplations in this book are designed to help us to feel deeply what is unfolding in the Act of Consecration of Man.

May my thinking live in the life of the
Holy Spirit.

The Act of Consecration of Man also demands that we school our thinking. As we sit in the service, we may find that a word or a phrase resonates in us particularly strongly, and we start to ponder on it. No sooner have we started down this track than we realise that a whole section of the Act of Consecration of Man has come to a close, whilst we were dwelling on one word. Or we may find that our thoughts have wandered and we are thinking about something completely different. As in the practice of meditation, it is not a matter of blaming ourselves for these lapses of concentration. Rather, we learn patiently to direct our attention back to what is happening at the altar right now.

A parable for the Offering

The pathway through the first two prayers of the Offering is echoed in the parable of the prodigal son (Luke 15:11–32). The younger of two sons asks his father for his share of the inheritance that will be due to him; taking it, he travels to a distant land where he squanders his money and experiences great poverty in a time of famine. Taking work as a swineherd and finding himself nearly starving, he finds his way 'into himself' where he discovers his will to become a worker on his father's estate. When he returns, his father greets him like a returning king or initiate. He seems to have become a person in a way that the older son, dutiful though he is, has not yet done.* The significance of his story is revealed when the father says of him, 'This brother of yours was dead and is alive again; he was lost and is found.'

The first prayer of the Offering invites us to recognise how far we have moved away from our origin in the divine and how much of the substance with which we were endowed we have squandered. The offering of willing, feeling and thinking stems from the intention no longer to be merely the recipients of grace, but to become collaborators with the divine world.

We all draw near to you in soul, O Christ, that you offer us with you.

* See Ravetz, *Free from Dogma*, p. 95.

After the cup has been offered up, we ask Christ to receive us into his offering of himself, which was not accomplished once and for all on Golgotha, but continues to this day. The Gospel of St John relates what happened when some representatives of the Jewish religious authorities hear that Jesus has performed a healing on the Sabbath day. Jesus' answer to their challenge only serves to deepen their outrage: 'My Father works until now, and so do I' (John 5:17 A). In the Jewish picture, creation was completed on the sixth day. The Sabbath was a day to rest and reflect on God's mighty deeds. Jesus' words seem to subvert this picture. The first creation has become the setting for a new one. In the Communion prayers in the Act of Consecration of Man we hear the repeated formula that Christ receives the 'life of the world' from the Father and 'makes it whole through the Spirit'. Creation is not yet finished. Its completion depends on the Holy Spirit, who works with the human spirit to advance it towards its goal.

The Letter to the Hebrews tells us that the old sacrificial rites prefigured the sacrifice of Christ. They were all fulfilled and superseded by Christ's sacrifice on Golgotha. If the sacrifices in pre-Christian times were attempts to reconnect the earthly world with the divine world, offering means now that the 'deed of life and death on Golgotha', as it is called in the Michaelmas prayer, becomes our reality here and now. Christ's sacrifice has been accomplished on Golgotha; its full realisation is still waiting for the end times. We are living in the time of tension between the 'is already' and 'is yet to come'.

The turning point of time becomes our present when we ask Christ to take our offering up into his self-offering. From this moment on, 'offering' or 'sacrifice' is spoken of in the Act of Consecration, we can be aware of two streams meeting: one that comes from the side of humanity and one that streams towards it from the divine world.

Spirits of creation

Angels, Archangels and Archai, the spirits of revelation, were at work in the Gospel Reading. In the Offering, we join the company of the spirits of creation. We follow a path through the elements of earth, water, air and fire, which the ancient world regarded as the fundamental constituents of the sense-perceptible world:

* The element of *earth* emerges when we notice, in the first prayer, the danger that our immortal being might be engulfed by our earthly nature.
* The element of *water*, which stands for everything that flows and connects, is present when the water and the wine become the bearers of the powers of our soul in the second prayer.
* The smoke of the incense makes the *air* visible; this receives the imprint of our words and bears them into the spiritual world.
* At the end of the Offering, the *fire* of love is kindled, in which new being comes to birth.

If we view the world as an undivided whole, everything that we perceive is the result of spiritual processes and the beings that stand behind them. The spirits of creation are at work in and through the elements. In the sacrificial fire, yet higher beings shine forth, engendering the new being that we pray for. The spirits closest to the throne of God, bear the name Seraphim, which is the Hebrew word for flame. As we pass from the Offering, the second part of the Act of Consecration of Man, to the Transubstantiation, we pass from the realm of creation into the realm of being itself. The fire of love is a revelation of the fiery heart of the divine love that lives at the core of all being (see Rev 4).

Heraclitus (*ca.* 535–475 BC), one of the earliest Greek philosophers, turned the ancient insight that everything came from fire and all the other elements are cooled, condensed fire, into the foundation of his philosophical system. Even in our technological age we can still experience the magical power of fire, which dissolves what has become solid in its living flames. Fire and the warmth that it creates are also fascinating because they are strongly related to our inner life. We can summon up an inner fire even on the coldest of days, if we fill ourselves with courage or moral resolve.

There is a striking parallel between these ancient insights and the ideas of modern physics. This manifests not in the details but in what we might call the gesture that they share. The picture of the beginning of the universe, which was mockingly called 'Big Bang' by a sceptic, is not really a bang but a sudden outpouring of heat. After the singularity – the still unexplained moment in which the world passes from potential to actual – comes an expansion of energy, which initially spreads in the form of heat or warmth. Only when this cools down do the subatomic particles begin to form. The elements, as chemistry knows them, condense even later, starting with hydrogen, the lightest of all.

In his descriptions of the origin of the world, Rudolf Steiner brought clear descriptions that shed light both on the old mythological images and on the insights of modern cosmology.* Spiritual warmth is the first manifestation of the divine will to create a world. The Thrones, who provide the basis for the work of the first hierarchy, as their name suggests, develop this inner, spiritual warmth, which they then offer up to yet higher beings, who at first accept their sacrifice. Then the process is interrupted. A part of the warmth falls away. Until now we can imagine the warmth that circulates between the beings as having a purely inner nature, just like the moral warmth that we feel inwardly. But now, some of the warmth has fallen out of the inner world of the divine. This becomes the basis of a world that exists over against the divine world and which can develop independently. This is the origin of the sense-perceptible world. If we live with the image that everything that our senses perceive is cooled, condensed warmth, we can enter the spirit of sacrifice in the ancient world. A divine fire dwells within the things of the

* Rudolf Steiner, *Esoteric Science,* Chapter 4.

sense-world, longing to be liberated. Once this power is set free, it can stream down as blessing.

In the Sacramental Consultation, which can serve as preparation for the Offering, the conversation that constitutes the first part of the sacrament leads over into a verse that describes a path of offering and receiving. Our thoughts are the first things to be offered up. Thoughts, as the end-product of thinking, start to fall out of alignment with reality the moment they are formed, because they are fixed and reality is constantly changing. It is easy to experience the blessing that flows when we make an offering of our thoughts: this is why a truly open conversation is so helpful. Fixed positions may come into movement; quite new ideas come towards us. All too often, we see thinking as juggling of thoughts that we have already thought, or heard from someone else. In a true conversation, we can experience living thinking.

The same applies to the area of feelings, if they have become too rigid. The will can also become too fixed, as for example when compulsive behaviour patterns impair our freedom to determine our own behaviour. One way of preparing for the Act of Consecration of Man is to work on particular things that we would like to entrust to the flames: fixed thoughts; suggestive feelings; compulsive patterns of behaviour. We can let them flow with the 'strayings, denials and weaknesses'. Then we can feel the freshness of the thinking, feeling and willing that turns to the Ground of the World with the pouring of the water and wine. We can feel how they in turn are taken up into sacrificial flame. For a moment we can embrace the emptiness that comes when we give everything over to the divine world: the emptiness that John Keats described as a positive capacity: negative capability.

When we reach the sacrificial fire at the end of the Offering, we have climbed the heavenly ladder all the way to the Seraphim (Gen 28:10–19). This is the moment when the Christmas prayer speaks of the 'song of sacrifice' of the heavenly hierarchies. First, in the Gospel Reading, the beings of the third hierarchy brought the Spirit close to us in revelation. The creator spirits accompanied us in the Offering. In the sacrificial fire we are drawn already into the activity of the beings of the first hierarchy, which unfolds in the Transubstantiation.

When we ponder the creation of the world we are confronted with a mystery: how can the timeless God who exists beyond space and time bring a world into being that is bound by time and space? The Act of Consecration of Man confronts us with a new mystery: how can a new world be born in the midst of the first creation? The sacrificial fire, which burns in what we have offered together with Christ, is the birthplace of a new, timeless being.

Contemplation: Fire

In the offering be born the fire of love, creative of being.

First we might recall experiences of outer fire. After a bonfire has been lit, the branches gradually catch fire and in the heart of the fire it seems as if they are melting into a molten core. Everything that was solid and fixed merges into the liquid of the glowing fire. From time to time the beams collapse and a stream of sparks rises to the sky.

Then, we may recall experiences in which we felt our inner fire: the fire of desire; the fire of love; the fire of righteous anger. We can allow these memories to light up in our soul. Then we let the details fade away so that only the essence of the inner warmth that we felt remains. We can send this warmth into our limbs; with time we realise that we can always call upon it, for example on a cold day, or when we are afraid.

Now we fill our souls with an imaginative picture: in the very heart of being itself lives the divine fire of love, which is the substance of the Seraphim.

In our imagination, we roll back everything that has arisen from this fire in the course of the creation and development of the world until we arrive at the state in which there is nothing but spiritual warmth. We imagine creation as the outpouring of the fire of love. Everything that we perceive, even the smallest particle, bears within it some of this fire.

In a further step we think of all the things that we have accumulated mentally: abilities, habits, preferences, also prejudices and one-sidedness. We choose which ones to carry to the spiritual fire at the altar, where they can be consumed. For a moment, we experience how our soul is empty: everything that was there has been burned up in the fire of love. Now, there is only the space where it once was. We hear the words resounding in this space:

In the offering be born the fire of love, creative of being.

3

The New Being:
Transubstantiation

Reality

At the time of the foundation of The Christian Community, ideas about the nature of reality were in a state of flux. From the beginning of the nineteenth century, the horizons of human knowledge had been expanding enormously. New insights into the nature of time came as a tremendous shock to the scholarly world. One challenge came from the realisation of the time-spans necessary for the geological ages and the evolution of life. How could such vast numbers of years be brought into harmony with the chronologies in the Old Testament? Then, ideas about the nature of space were changed radically in the early years of the twentieth century by Einstein's theory of relativity. The existence of galaxies beyond our own was postulated and then borne out by further research, which in turn led to the image of the expanding universe. In the quantum realm, the breakthrough came with the idea of a world in which matter – until then the solid foundation of things – came to be seen as the vibrations of forces in constant flux. The absolute boundary between observers and the world outside them also seemed to dissolve when experiments in quantum physics demonstrated that the question with which we approach reality changes the reality we experience.

If at the beginning of the twentieth century it was still regarded as certain that the world was an eternally closed system in which nothing could break the chain of cause and effect, by the middle of the century, physicists generally accepted that the universe had a beginning in which it had emerged from a completely different state, in which quite different laws applied. This loosened the straitjacket of mechanistic materialism.

The founders of The Christian Community were inspired by the possibility of developing yet deeper insights into the origin of the universe through their encounter with Rudolf Steiner's work. His research results and the methods of inner, meditative inquiry which he taught make it possible to bridge the gap between the world of scientific knowledge and spiritual reality by undergoing a rigorous path of inner schooling. In the lectures that Steiner gave to help with the founding of The Christian Community, he made it clear that a modern religious life is only possible if we see the world without divisions. Steiner summed this up in the challenging question, can our prayers have a real effect? Only if we can answer this question positively with clear thinking can we integrate something like the transformation of bread and wine into our world system.

The world of thought that was passing away at the beginning of the twentieth century did not offer this possibility. Since the Middle Ages, the Catholic Church has taught that a kind of miracle occurs in transubstantiation, in which the underlying nature (in philosophical language: substance) of bread and wine is exchanged with that of the body and blood of Christ while their external qualities of appearance, smell, taste and so on (the philosophical term is 'accidents') are preserved. Those who could not accept this dogmatic definition might look upon the Eucharist as a symbol of Jesus' love for us – not 'real', but meaningful for our inner world of experience.

Our challenge is to find a way of thinking that supports the experiences we can have in the Act of Consecration of Man. In the twentieth century, some theologians strove to articulate their experience of a Christ who was deeply involved in the process of the world's evolution in a way that took the great changes in physics and philosophy into account. Teilhard de Chardin famously developed his idea of the 'Omega Point', the ultimate destination of the universe. For him, Christ's death and resurrection had restored the earth to its place in cosmic evolution and implanted within it the possibility that it might find its fulfilment. Taking such thoughts together with the insights of Rudolf Steiner, the importance of Christ's life in the evolution of the world becomes clear. When Christ's blood impregnated the earth and his body was laid in the womb of her grave, the earth was permeated with divine substance. The resurrection is a foretaste of the future of the earth, when earthly substance will have been so permeated with God's love that it becomes something quite new and all earthly experience is gathered up into a new kind of being.

Re-presenting

Let live... in this Christ-offering the body
and the blood of your son, who has his
being in love.

The prologue of the Gospel of St John describes how the divine word, the creator of all that is, becomes a human being on the earth. Christ enters step by step into earthly reality. This process could be called the original sacrament: the highest spiritual reality takes on sense-perceptible form. Ever and again, Jesus foretells the bitter consequences of his decision to unite with human existence – a decision that stems from his love for human beings (see for instance, Mark 8:31ff; 9:30f and 10:33f). This decision culminates at the Last Supper when he shares his body and blood with the disciples in the form of the bread and the wine. Following this, he has to experience the utter isolation of human existence in the Garden of Gethsemane (see for example Luke 22:42).

Christ's presence in the elements of bread and wine in the Last Supper becomes present for us in the heart of the Act of Consecration of Man. In the prayers preparing the Gospel Reading, we already lived into the sphere of Christ's life in which his words and deeds live on. Now this life unites with our earthly being in a new way. The words which recall the love of Christ that led to his suffering and death are the portal to experiencing this new being. Having spoken these words, the celebrant takes first the bread and then the cup as she speaks words which narrate the actions of the Lord's Supper. The priest kneels down, breaks the bread and draws three crosses over the cup and the paten, the plate that holds the bread. The words and deeds of the Last Supper become our present experience. We have left the time which can be measured and which, starting with creation, runs from the past to the future (in Greek, *chronos*). We enter the time of potential and fulfilment, the time of which John the Baptist spoke: 'The time [*kairos*] is fulfilled, the kingdom of God is at hand' (Mark 1:15 A).

In the Offering we prayed that our soul-offering might be taken up into Christ's sacrificial offering. In the Transubstantiation, we ask that the body and blood of Christ may *live* in the offering. A first stage in the changing of bread and wine seems to have taken place here: our offering has been ensouled and is now enlivened by Christ. The next step takes place when the bread is broken and Christ invites us, together with his disciples, to receive body and blood with the bread and the wine. The substances become the bearers of the body and the blood.

In the Gospel of Luke, after the sharing of the bread and wine, Jesus tells the disciples: 'Do this in remembrance of me' (Luke 22:19). This translation of the Greek word *anamimnesko* runs the risk of making the celebration of the Lord's Supper nothing more than a reminder of something from the past, as it is understood in some Protestant churches. We can also hear it differently: bring the past into the present; let it become your present; let it become a living reality in the midst of your soul!

A member once described how during the Transubstantiation, he noticed that he was wearing his watch when it accidentally slipped from under his sleeve and the dial caught his eye. This was an experience that he did not wish to repeat; nevertheless, it was interesting because his shock revealed the ideas which he was unconsciously holding about the passing of time during the Act of Consecration of Man. Glancing at his watch, he realised that he would have expected either that it would have stopped, or that the hands would be moving so fast that they pointed at all the numbers at once. Such an experience points to the quality of the time that we are now entering.

In the Apocalypse the Christ says of himself: 'I am the Alpha and the Omega, world-origin and world-purpose.' (Rev 22:13 A). The Transubstantiation not only connects the past event of the Lord's Supper with our experience in the here and now; it is a prophetic embodiment of a future reality. Bread and wine light up as icons for the whole earth, which is destined to be completely permeated by Christ.

Contemplation: The Gift

We have received a gift from our friend who lives far away. She has chosen a beautiful book for us, written an inscription, wrapped it carefully and taken the time to post it to us. Opening the parcel, we wonder whether the postage cost more than the present itself. We wonder for a moment whether it would have been better if she had sent us a gift voucher. Then we could have bought something near to home, and saved her the trouble and expense of posting it. However, we realise that the gift has a value that goes far beyond what it cost. It embodies her love, whose traces it bears in the inscription. Years later, we take the book down from the shelf and are reminded of the love that it embodies.

One definition of a sacrament is 'a visible sign of an invisible grace'. The book that was given to us is a visible embodiment of the invisible love of our friend. If a human being with all their limitations can permeate a common object with their love so that it serves as a sign of this love for years to come, can we imagine how much more Christ could do when he gave his disciples the gift of bread and wine?

Working with the methods outlined above (see pages 39f) we imagine the moment when Christ shared out the bread and the wine at the Last Supper (see Matt. 26:17–30, Mark 14:12–26, Luke 22:7–39 and John 13:1–17:26). The power of his love permeates the bread and wine through and through so that they become part of his whole embodied existence: so that they are included in his body and blood.

Knowing

Take this into your thinking.

In the first centuries of the church, what happened in the Transubstantiation was hardly discussed. The experience of receiving communion must have been so powerful that it was not necessary to speculate about how it came about. Towards the turn of the first millennium, theologians turned to the question of what we might mean when we speak of bread and wine as the body and blood of Christ. Have they *really* changed? Or are they merely symbols that we invest with meaning, without their changing objectively at all?

Many people feel moved to come forward and receive communion long before they have found thoughts with which to understand it. There, they experience a deeper, intuitive knowing, which is often wiser than our intellect. In a book such as this, we are not seeking explanations. However, if we wish to deepen our experiences for ourselves or make them accessible to others, it is helpful if we can reflect upon what we have experienced. Are there thoughts that can encompass the reality that bread and wine become part of a new being, a new nature, permeated by Christ? Such thinking will lead us to further questions, not deliver a simple, logical answer, which would bring to an end our own pondering on our experiences.

As so often, we move in a spectrum of possibilities that lives between two extremes, each of which on its own loses touch with the reality that we cannot fully describe. If the change in the bread and wine is nothing more than a symbol, does this do justice to our experiences during communion, when we may feel touched by a higher reality? On the other hand, if the change could be detected under a microscope or by chemical analysis, would this almost be *too* real?

The idea that inner values and experiences belong to an utterly different part of reality from outer, objective reality belongs to an old picture that was replaced during the twentieth century, as we have seen above in relation to quantum mechanics. In the realm of inorganic nature, research into water crystallisation has shown that inner states can have a significant effect on the growth of crystal forms.* Viktor Frankl was the first to describe on a psychological level how our experience of reality depends on how we relate to it. In our dealings with other human beings, most strikingly with children, we can prevent or promote their unfolding by the way that we look at them. This means that we have the power to change more than

* See, for example, Bernd Kröplin and Regine C. Henschel, *Water and its Memory*, Kindle 2017. Also Andreas Schulz, *Water Crystals*, Floris Books 2005, or Mararu Emoto, *The Message from Water*, Hado, Japan 2001.

merely our own experience: my way of seeing the child can further or hinder the child's development and growth.

This helps us to understand the uniquely human contribution to the Offering, which makes the water and wine into bearers of the highest forces of our souls. A next step takes place in the Transubstantiation when we pray that the Risen One might permeate the bread and wine with life. At a later stage, we pray that Christ may 'hold sway' in bread and wine. Can we imagine here that the living substance of the resurrection, which permeated the earth following the crucifixion, now becomes more active in the substances? Then we might conceive how earthly substances could become bearers of spiritual powers.

At the climax of the Transubstantiation, the service takes us a step further, when we pray that the bread and the wine might *be* body and blood themselves. It is good to contemplate the progression here. Is there a difference when we say that one thing has changed *into* another? The service itself corrects us if we start to think of the kind of change that we are used to in our everyday life, such as coal changing into ash. If it were this kind of change, we would expect that from now we would always speak of body and blood and not of bread and wine. However, the service moves between the two.

Clearly, the new way of being of bread and wine as body and blood is radically different from the way in which the book which you are holding *is,* or of the desk at which I am writing *is.* The book and the desk, like all the other objects around us, exist because of a long chain of past causes that have ended in this moment. When we think about even the simplest objects and try to follow the chain of causes backwards, we can grow almost dizzy. Before I could buy the desk, it had to be designed, manufactured and marketed. Before that could happen, the trees had to grow. Before that, human culture had to develop the concepts of writing, and of forestry. Before that, the world had to evolve to the point that there were trees, and humans. In the end, whatever we look at has its origin in the beginning of things, the primordial moment of creation. The way we speak of things that have come into being like this is expressed in what scholars of language call the indicative mood: *this is my desk.* When we refer to the bread and wine, we are in a different 'mood': the mood expressed by 'let the bread be ...' In grammar, such moods are called *irrealis* – unreal. This demonstrates the challenge we face when we try to comprehend that this new reality might be as real as the reality of the desk.

At the altar, bread and wine *may be* body and blood, because they are joined to a stream of causality that works from the future into the present. We can grasp the idea of a cause that exists in the future if we look again at the example of the desk. The wood that was needed to make it and the factory where it was shaped already existed before it was designed. However, when someone decided to create the desk, it was then a future reality. Only the designer's intuition of the form of the desk could organise the wood, metal and plastic that were needed to create it. This is the 'final' cause, the direction towards which things were tending, which Aristotle described. Twentieth century thinkers such as Teilhard de Chardin and others had an inkling of this causality. There have been great debates about how the idea of a final cause applies to the natural world, as it so clearly does to the world of things made by human beings. Clearly, the 'design' of the world is different from the blueprint that the designer gives to a factory, because it is constantly being reshaped to take account of the free decisions of human beings. Charles Taylor describes the gentle action of the Holy Spirit in the tendency of creation to move towards greater complexity, individuation, and self-giving love. The Spirit cannot compel us, because it is respectful of human freedom. Instead, it 'allures' us towards the future that is beckoning to us.

St Paul describes the future direction, the 'final cause' of the created world in his Letter to the Ephesians (1:9f):

[God the Father] made known to us the mystery
of his will according to his good pleasure, which he
purposed in Christ, to be put into effect when the
times reach their fulfilment – to bring unity to all
things in heaven and on earth under Christ.

Perhaps this feels as if it takes us too far in one direction, as though the change being described is so real that it could be observed if bread and wine were examined under laboratory conditions. A scientific laboratory is designed for a particular way of looking, concentrating on material causes. Perhaps an alchemist's laboratory, which was a place for prayer and meditation as much as for scientific investigation, would have been better suited to this task.

Another common experience may help us to understand this: human beings constantly bestow new meaning on the things around us. The earliest human beings took pigment and scraped it onto cave walls to embody the forces of nature that they worked with outside; we shape a mound of stones or plant a rose and call it a memorial. We may take some planks and cloths and declare that this will be an altar. Of course, there are limitations to this: only our continuing attention will maintain the new meaning that we have given, as we see when archaeologists excavate long-forgotten objects whose use they can only guess at.

Additionally, we are free to give meaning that is in alignment with the origin and destination of the world, or to do it arbitrarily. Many philosophers of the sixties and seventies insisted that meaning was nothing but a social construct. They taught us to be suspicious of any authority that claimed to control meaning, whether that be a church or a political authority. They made it clear that every human being has to take responsibility for creating the meaning that they experience. The artist Marcel Duchamp demonstrated memorably with his artwork, *The Urinal*. He elevated this most everyday of objects into a work of art by placing it in an art gallery in order to make us aware that in our current age, we are free to give meaning however we wish.

Your spirit's power of grace work earthward as this offering strives heavenward.

The Act of Consecration of Man describes a journey through which the congregation itself develops the capacity to 'know Christ in freedom'. The one heart and one soul that has formed through the celebration develop the capacity to think and to know. When we pray that bread and wine might *be* body and blood, we take on a task of cognition: from now on, we will recognise in them the future reality that they embody. The prayer spoken in the moment before the climax of the Transubstantiation joins us to the working of the Holy Spirit, the great connector.* The spirit assures us that our recognition of this new reality is no arbitrary decision of our own. Our spirit-drenched knowing, as it is described in the Trinity Epistle, encompasses the new being: the body and blood of Christ in their new reality. The words, 'let ... be,' mark the moment of joining: spirit streams down to the earth as grace and connects earthly substances to their destination. The spirit in us looks up to the changing and recognises the new being. Spirit joins with spirit in the transubstantiation and heals the divided world.

A member once described how while waiting to receive communion he had the insight that he expressed in the words: 'This is this'. He found in himself a capacity to know, which went far deeper than the familiar, intellectual act of knowing. He knew with the deepest certainty that in the communion the source of our being, Christ's body and blood, is given to us. Another member told us how, at the moment when the bread and wine were held up, she had experienced a kind of inversion of her consciousness. Bands of light streamed out from the altar, a little like the ribbons that radiate from the maypole. She felt connected to all these ribbons as if her consciousness were spread through

* See Ravetz, *Free from Dogma*, p. 67.

the whole church. She was filled with conviction: the light which surrounds me here is the real being, which underlies my everyday reality. What I see with my eyes is only the outside of reality.

Looking with the eyes of hierarchies

When we pray at the end of the Transubstantiation that bread and wine might be the body and blood of Christ, then we have entered the sphere of the 'timeless' being for which we prayed at the end of the Offering. We have already tried to imagine the consciousness of the Angels, Archangels and Archai. Living with the thought that there are such beings who behold us from a higher perspective can be helpful when we reflect on the events of our own lives and of human history. We can use the same imaginative leap in relation to yet higher ranks of the hierarchies. Of course, it is far harder to feel our way into the mind of the Thrones than that of our Angel. Nevertheless, we know the fire of love that fills us when we feel called to be creative, whether that be in artistic creation or in loving deeds that enable others. This gives us a point of connection to beings whose creative fire is so great that they can beget worlds. The Seraphim, whose very name embodies the fiery origin of the universe, look upon the earth as the place where the goal of the world will be fulfilled. They long to witness human beings in their loving co-creation. The purpose of the incarnation of Christ is to preserve this possibility. He permeates Jesus of Nazareth's human nature so that he can create a new kind of human nature in the resurrection. This is what St Paul calls the Second Adam, the new human being.

What took place in Jesus of Nazareth seeks to become universal. The Transubstantiation is destined in the end to encompass the whole earth.

Contemplation: Thinking the Transubstantiation

Take this into your thinking.

The Act of Consecration of Man itself challenges us to develop a way of thinking that can live into its reality. It even describes how the events of Christ's passion and death will start to 'think in us'. This will not be analytical thinking, nor will it try to bring our questioning to an end. For anyone who would like to rise to this challenge, I have summarised some of the thoughts that we have looked at so far, which may be of help in such reverential explorations:

* The universe had a beginning before which completely different laws held sway than those which are now considered universal and unchangeable. It passed from this time of pure potential to our world of incredible richness and diversity through the divine word, the same being who as Jesus Christ invites us to his table in the Act of Consecration of Man.

* In the sacrificial flame at the end of the Offering, we experience a foretaste of the end-times when everything that has come into being since Creation will pass back into pure potentiality, enriched by all the experiences that have been accumulated in its journey into actuality. We are drawn into the mystery of the new being that will emerge within our earthly experience. This new being is the earth permeated by Christ through and through.
* In the Transubstantiation, Christ's deed of love at the Last Supper becomes our present reality.
* The division into an outer world of objective facts and an inner world of experience is a construct of a particular consciousness that does not correspond to reality. We are co-creators of the reality that we experience.
* Our efforts to ponder what happens at the altar are completed through the working of the Holy Spirit and our co-celebrants in the congregation.

We could choose any one of these thoughts to contemplate in our own way; we could then deepen it in feeling, as we described in relation to the Lectio Divina above. We could in turn develop a prayerful mood, praying that we might take part more consciously and actively when we next attend the Act of Consecration of Man.

The Lord's Prayer

As our relationship with the Act of Consecration of Man deepens, we may find that our experience of the Lord's Prayer can change. The Act of Consecration of Man embodies what we pray for in the Lord's Prayer.

Living with the gospels is a way of 'hallowing' the word of God, allowing it to unfold its potential within us. Gradually the experience can grow in us that every thought is a part of the name of God.

When we act in alignment with the heavenly world we can experience that the kingdom – the state in which earthly reality is united again with its source and destination – approaches us. In the Offering we have the opportunity to practise this when we align ourselves to the Christ's offering.

In the Transubstantiation, we experience for a moment the result of this alignment, when the ultimate will of the divine world for the earth is revealed: that it should become the body and blood of Christ.

Following this, our prayer for true nourishment has a special resonance.

As we approach communion, we have to confront the reality of temptation and debt.

Finally, we realise that we cannot overcome the powers

of the adversaries on our own. Without relinquishing responsibility for our actions, we realise that only the help of the spiritual world can help us on our path.

4

Communion

Encounter

Since time immemorial, human beings have sought to commune with the spiritual world through ritual meals. The first three parts of the Act of Consecration of Man serve to prepare the meal that we share with the divine world. Every Gospel Reading announces that Christ is coming, as healer, teacher or radical transformer of human experience. In the Offering, we make space in our soul to welcome the guest. When a beloved friend whom we have not seen for many years comes to visit, we may find that we both fall silent for a moment when we first meet. The very fact of being together makes all the difference. In the silent moments in the heart of the Transubstantiation we can experience the same quality of encounter. All of this prepares us for the meal that we share with Christ. When we share a meal with our friends, we find nourishment beyond the food that we eat: the encounter itself feeds us. What we share becomes a part of us.

The prayers that prepare the Communion show the many-sided effects of the encounter with Christ.

* It gives us peace.
* It strengthens the forces that keep us alive.
* It strengthens that part of us that endures beyond death.
* It strengthens us against the attack of adversary forces.
* It is medicine that heals us from the 'sickness of sin' by permeating our entire being.

Peace with the world

I stand at peace with the world.

In the farewell discourses (John 14–17), Jesus prepares his disciples for the trials they will have to face in the world, and comforts them: 'But be not afraid: I have overcome the world' (John 16:33 A). Christ holds the powers in check that seek to tear us out of our connection with the Ground of Being. His descent into the depths of earthly experience, culminating in the crucifixion, exposes him to the dimensions of experience that are furthest from the divine world (compare the Creed of The Christian Community). His peace with the world stems from his affirmation of the world with all its darkness.

In the face of the difficulties and darkness with which the world confronts us, we face a dual temptation: we can allow ourselves to be crushed by the challenges we face and give up, or we may seek to distance ourselves from them. Whenever we turn away from the dark sides of world history and current events or from our own unacknowledged difficult sides, we divide the world into two parts. The first sentence of the Creed challenges us to overcome such divisions, when it affirms the unity of reality and experience. The peace which is promised to us in Communion does not represent a standstill: it is the promise of the strengthening of the middle that we continually find and lose between the extremes.

Sickness of Sin

Trees and animals have no problem. God makes them what they are without consulting them, and they are perfectly satisfied. With us it is different. God leaves us free to be whatever we like. We can be ourselves or not, as we please. We are at liberty to be real, or to be unreal. We may be true or false, the choice is ours. We may wear now one mask and now another, and never, if we so desire, appear with our own true face. But we cannot make these choices with impunity. Causes have effects, and if we lie to ourselves and to others, then we cannot expect to find truth and reality whenever we happen to want them. If we have chosen the way of falsity we must not be surprised that truth eludes us when we finally come to need it! Our vocation is not simply to *be*, but to work together with God in the creation of our own life, our own identity, our own destiny.
(Thomas Merton, *New Seeds of Contemplation*, New Directions, New York 2007)

As we have seen in our approach to the Offering, we live in a creative tension between our experience of ourselves with all of our limitations and shortcomings and our sense that we may become far greater than this. When we look back on our lives, we will probably find that we have not accomplished all of the goals that we set ourselves; indeed, we may have completely missed some of them. We will probably remember moments when we were asked to help with words or deeds, and how we squandered those opportunities. We may also become mindful of moments when someone tried to help us without our noticing. We see that there were moments when love was needed and we were not able to give it; in others, love was offered and we were too blind or too proud to accept it. We may notice that we fall into old habits or compulsions that we thought we had left behind.

All of this shows that we are constantly engaged in the work of transforming ourselves. We are co-creators of our identity and our destiny, as Thomas Merton says. If simply wishing to change were enough to bring about the change on its own, matters would be easy. But when we try to change our character or our behaviour in one or the other regard, again and again we encounter layers of our being that resist this transformation. In the Creed, this problem, which is deeply rooted in our constitution, is called 'the sickness of sin of the bodily nature of man.' 'Bodily' here has a wider meaning than just 'physical'. The soul also has a kind of body, which we know as our psychological make-up. Beneath this, patterns of behaviour and habits are imprinted in forms that change our constitution.

If we wish to become responsible for our actions as free human beings we need to recognise the ways in which the sickness of sin limits our freedom to determine our course in life. The pioneers of the twelve-step programmes, which are used by Alcoholics Anonymous and people who suffer from many other types of addiction, recognised this. The first step is to recognise that we cannot solve our problem alone and to surrender to a higher power (the programme is not religious, so the identity of that power is left open). In a seeming contradiction, along with this surrender, one takes full responsibility for what one has done while one was 'in the grip of addiction'. It can be breathtaking to witness the honesty of people who have reached a point in their life where they had to acknowledge this.

The term 'sickness of sin' is a mirror in which we can find a kind of self-diagnosis. It can trigger powerful reactions in us, which themselves reveal something about the consequences of this condition. On the one hand it may wound our vanity to see ourselves as sick and in need of healing. On the other hand, we may feel crushed by this description of ourselves. Here we experience the dual nature of the powers whose task it is to tempt us from the middle, where our freedom lies. One force always lures us into 'too much', into overestimating our capabilities, our freedom. The other pulls us down and threatens to crush us under the weight of earthly necessity. In the prayers at Christmastime we experience how Christ brings healing to a humanity which is caught between the 'vain show of illusion' and the 'senses' unworthy craving'. Even if we do not need the intensive help of a twelve-step programme, a little self-reflection shows how often we fall prey to one or the other extreme.

A look at what is expressed with the old words 'virtue' and 'vice' can help us with our self-diagnosis. For example: the opposite of generosity is clearly meanness. But what about extravagance? If at the end of the month I can't provide for my family because I was too generous with everyone who asked, I can't call that a virtue. Between avarice and waste there is a quality of the middle that is made up of generosity moderated by prudence.

Or to take another example: Everyone will acknowledge that boastfulness is not a desirable attitude. Perhaps the opposite would be self-abasement. What would be the quality of the middle? Modest self-confidence? A pride in success that does not relate to me?

All such questions, which were formulated already by Aristotle, give us an instrument to recognise the consequences of the 'sickness of sin' within us. We need to develop patience and honesty if we want to gain such self-knowledge. The path itself confronts us with adversaries who prevent us from developing an honest view of our situation. The struggle for an objective picture can become a prayer that we may be granted greater insight. The conversation that constitutes the first part of the Sacramental Consultation can be a help here. Speaking about my situation before Christ can bring courage and clarity.

The Passiontide prayers take us from the empty heart to the experience of the fire of shame in the heart. In our contemplation of this movement we have already looked at repentance. Only when we have allowed ourselves to feel deeply the consequences of our state of soul and looked steadily at their causes does self-knowledge ripen into a resolve to tackle these destructive patterns, whilst acknowledging that the struggle will be lifelong. The Communion does not relieve us of this responsibility, but it promises help in strengthening our middle.

Making whole

... the medicine that makes whole.

The church grew out of the experience that the incarnation of Christ has fundamentally changed the situation of humanity.* This is summed up in the image of 'salvation', a word that preserves one of the ancient root-words of the Indo-European languages: *sol,* which means whole or preserved. The writers of the New Testament use this word in a number of different ways. It can mean rescue or deliverance from a physical danger or illness. It can mean liberation from demonic possession. It is used most frequently of all in relation to our liberation from sin. The relationship between these images becomes clear if we ponder on the image of sin as sickness, as our Creed describes it. Our descent into one-sidedness necessarily leads us away from our original wholeness. Deliverance from the consequences of sin is restoration and healing.

The healing of the sickness of sin did not happen once and for all: it was inaugurated as a possibility through the death and resurrection of Christ. Since then, it seeks to permeate the whole of reality. In the Last Supper, Christ establishes a new relationship between human beings

* Compare Ravetz, *The Incarnation,* p. 80.

and the divine world. The apostles are given the task of continuing this relationship by celebrating the Eucharist, the encounter with Christ, through bread and wine. For the earliest theologians, there was no great difference between their encounter with Christ at the Lord's Supper and the kind of encounter that the disciples had with Jesus after the Resurrection.

The Gospels show the many facets of Christ's healing power.

❋ He gives us a new orientation by showing new possibilities of being human. The power of this example can be seen in the stories of the martyrs, beginning with Stephen (Acts 7:54–60).
❋ He strengthens our middle, allowing us to develop freedom between the extremes that embody the adversary powers. We can see this in the story of the man possessed by demons (Mark 5:1–20). The two moments of transformation in the story of the woman caught committing adultery (John 8) demonstrate this too: those who are possessed with a stony spirit of justice and vengeance find the mirror of their conscience, whilst the woman who has lost herself in passion is empowered to continue on her path in life with a new attention to her responsibility for her actions.

* He heals physical diseases by strengthening the innermost self of the other in such a way that the whole person can be permeated by his power.

Each of these aspects can be found in the Act of Consecration of Man.

* The stories of the life of Christ in the Gospel Reading place archetypes of the new humanity in our soul. This experience is intensified in the Transubstantiation, when the gospel of the Lord's Supper is enacted before our eyes.
* In the Offering we start on a journey towards the healing of our middle, when we recognise the consequences of the sickness of sin in our strayings, denials and weaknesses and then offer up the forces of our soul to the higher world.
* In the Communion, we receive Christ's body and blood as the medicine that makes whole. The intimate process of receiving communion heals an aspect of our isolation. We stand with our mouths open, completely receptive for the gift of the spiritual world. The priest comes far closer than we would normally allow someone to approach us; their fingers touch us.

A member once described an experience that she had after the Act of Consecration of Man had finished. She had been waiting in the foyer to attend to something else, so she saw the congregation emerging from the chapel. People's faces were illumined. For a few moments, they seemed to be freed from their everyday concerns. They were surrounded by a gentle glow. Without putting ourselves under pressure to have deep experiences (which usually chases such experiences away!) it can be valuable if in the evening we create a quiet listening space to allow any subtle experiences to resound in us – for example, by looking back on what we experienced at the altar that morning.

Contemplation: New Life

... that the sickness of sin be healed.

We all have many experiences on which we can draw if we want to contemplate the experience of healing. Here are a few examples that might inspire personal reflection:

* After a long illness, we feel the gradual return of our energy and vitality.
* We have been alienated from someone whom we loved for years. All attempts at reconciliation changed nothing: we seemed doomed to remain in conflict. One day, a message comes – perhaps something as brief as a text message – and we know: life is flowing between us again!
* We were in a conflict and had reached the point of giving up. The mood of despair suddenly changed when someone found the courage to break through the seemingly hopeless situation with a new word that embodied a new insight.
* In an abandoned factory or industrialised area, we see the power of nature to regenerate. The stones are lifted by sprouting saplings; ivy pulls

down the old walls. Even pools of waste have been taken over by particularly vivid vegetation.

In addition to personal memories, there are other sources:

* The Bible contains many accounts of life emerging from death, most obviously in the raisings from the dead and the healings in the Old Testament and the Gospels. The inner experiences described in the Psalms and the Book of Job foreshadow the mystical experience of death and new life in Christ that Paul describes (1Kings 17:17–24; Mark 5:21–43; John 11; Rom 6:1–14; Gal 2:19–22). We could work with any of the methods outlined above to bring these alive within our soul. (see the section 'Bringing the gospel to life within', p. 39 above).
* Reports of so-called near-death experiences.*

We allow the feelings that the pictures from memory and other sources evoke to fill our souls before we let them fade away so that we can attend to

* See, for instance, George G. Ritchie and Elizabeth Sherrill, *Return from Tomorrow,* or Raymond Moody, *Life after Life.*

the space that is left. We could let the word 'healing' resound in that space. In this mood, we might recall the last time we took communion and prepare ourselves for the next time we will receive it.

Conclusion: Uniting with the world's evolving

> Like his relationship to his work partner, man's
> relationship to God derives from the work they
> do together. Rather than shutting out the world to
> delve into each other's depths the way adolescent
> lovers do, God and men find joy together in doing
> a common task.
> (Harvey Cox, *The Secular City*, quoted in
> *The Go-Between God*, p. 37)

The Ordination of priests in The Christian Community
is integrated into a special Act of Consecration of Man,
in the course of which the candidates are given what they
need to take up their role as priests at the altar. Beyond the
consecration of the human being, which we all take part
in, they are consecrated for priesthood. We could conclude
from this that every Act of Consecration of Man is a kind
of Ordination into the 'priesthood of all believers' (Rev 1:6).
The aim of this universal priesthood is to transform our
whole life into an act of consecration. We can see this in
relation to the four parts of the Act of Consecration of Man.

﹡ We have already discussed the task that we are given at
Easter to proclaim Christ as the 'meaning of the earth'.
As we have seen, this does not necessarily mean talking

a lot about Jesus or God. In many situations, however, it is not what we say that counts: actions often speak far louder than words. To give one example: our interest in our fellow human beings is a living witness to our conviction that every human destiny has a meaning.

✳ The attitude that we develop in the Offering can live on in our approach to life. Are we prepared to bring fixed ideas into movement? Where do we find meaning and purpose in life? Do we place our lives in relation to the greatest context, the ultimate Ground of Being itself?

✳ Dealing with everyday experiences in such a way that they become transparent for higher worlds brings us close to the sphere of the Transubstantiation. Can we create moments of silence in which the presence of Christ can become part of our present? Can we feel that what we do, we do with and for Christ, so that he is part of our life, as he promised: 'Where two or three are gathered in my name, there am I among them' (Matt. 18:20 A)?

The aim of The Christian Community and the Act of Consecration of Man is not to keep people in the church for as long as possible. The Christian Community wants to serve the world by sending out into the world those who bear Christ within themselves. Our celebration in community is intended to strengthen us for this priestly service in the world. This is the thought behind Paul's beautiful words:

> We know that the whole creation has been groaning in labour pains until now; and not only the creation, but we ourselves, who have the first fruits of the Spirit, groan inwardly while we wait for adoption, the redemption of our bodies. (Rom 8:22f A).

Contemplation: Water of life

Then the angel showed me the river of the water of life, as clear as crystal, flowing from the throne of God and of the Lamb (Rev 22:1).

The water of life embodies the forces that can re-enliven the existence of the earth. To prepare for a contemplation of how this water flows through the Act of Consecration of Man, we can think of all the areas of life that need re-enlivening:

❋ We are growing increasingly aware of the fragile balances that sustain life on earth and how they are under threat through human activity. Beyond the action necessary to prevent pollution and undo the damage that has been done through human activity, we know that the way human beings do their work makes a difference to the world of nature. When we come to a place that has been cared for in a prayerful way, we can experience the special atmosphere that has been created.

❋ Our culture is – perhaps uniquely in world history – thrown back on purely human resources. In earlier times, divine wisdom inspired culture to a greater or lesser degree. Our journey towards freedom has led to a situation in which there is no greater taboo in some circles than to speak of God or of meaning.

* Politically, we can see a kind of vacuum that has opened up since the dominant ideologies of the twentieth century have run out of steam. How can we create a society that fosters individual initiative and responsibility whilst demonstrating compassion for the less able?

* It can feel as if we are in the grasp of a world-system, a kind of intelligence which only a few or perhaps no-one really wants, but no-one can resist. As more and more of the infrastructure on which our civilisation depends is run by artificial intelligence, this trend will only increase.

In these and many other areas, there is much that can give us cause for concern. If we can bear to look at this levelly, we may also notice the upsurge of new life, often arising from the awareness of the dangers that we face.

All of this could flow into a contemplation of the Act of Consecration of Man.

Behind the altar, a great waterfall streams down. When the priest turns around and says, 'Christ in you,' this living water flows through the priest, through the congregation and out into the world. Outside, the earth has dried up like a riverbed in a time of drought. The water of life from behind the altar flows into the cracks in the ground and makes it moist again, so that new life can take hold. When we receive communion, the water drenches us through and through. Turning round to make our way back to our seats, and later to leave the church to go back into our daily life, we are aware of the water of life flowing through us. The world is parched and in desperate need; we can bring it the water that will bring it to life.

After the concluding words of the Act of Consecration of Man have echoed away, we feel our calling to bear the water of life out into the world, into all areas of our life, into every encounter, every thought, everything we touch and see.

Floris
Books

For news on all our **latest books**,
and to receive **exclusive discounts**,
join our mailing list at:

florisbooks.co.uk

Plus subscribers get a FREE book
with every online order!

We will never pass your details to anyone else.